IMAGES
of America

MOORESTOWN

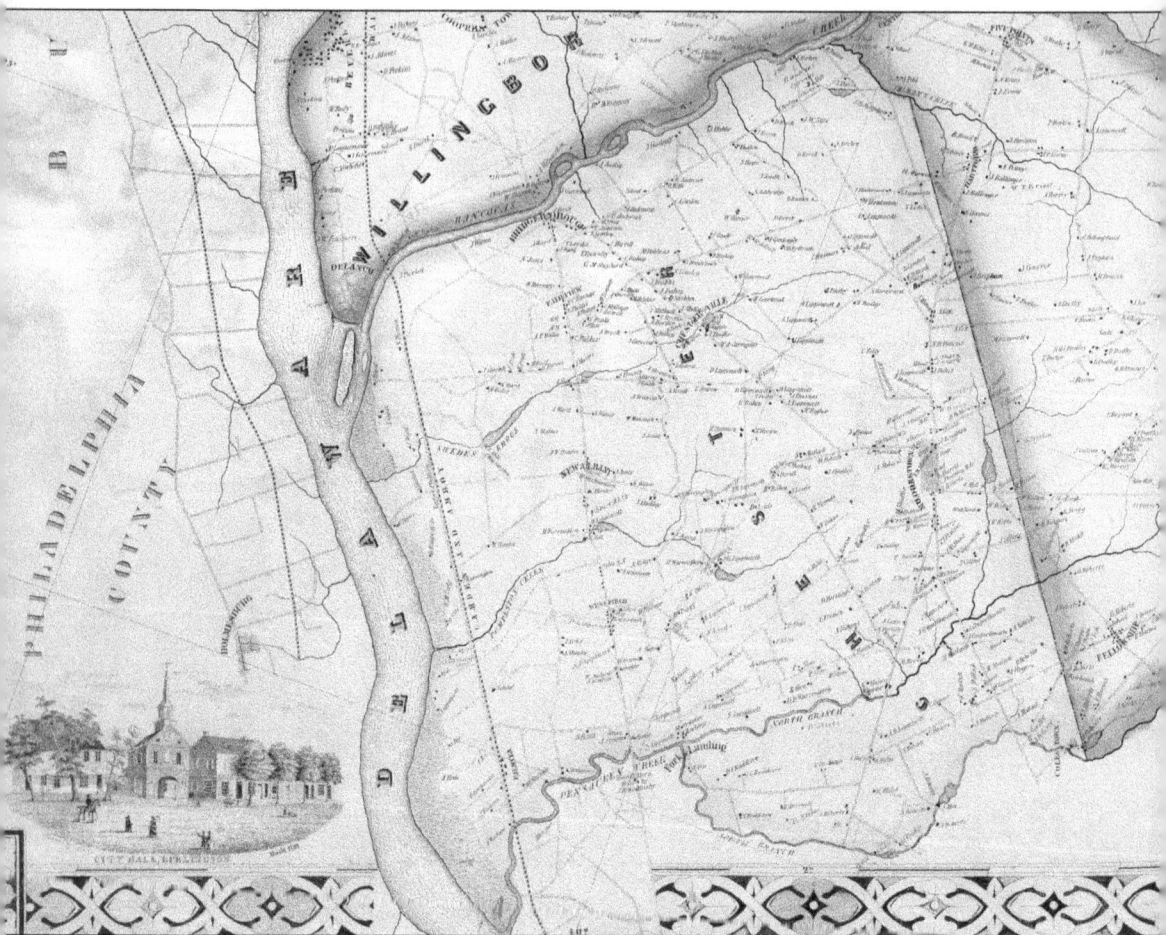

Incorporated on November 6, 1688, Chester Township originally included all the territory east of the Delaware River, from the south side of the Rancocas Creek to the south branch of the Pennsauken Creek and east into what is now Mount Laurel and Cherry Hill. The western section became Cinnaminson Township in 1860, and in 1922, Moorestown officially separated from Chester Township, which changed its name to Maple Shade in 1945. This 1849 map of Burlington County was published in Philadelphia by Smith & Wistar. (Courtesy of Library of Congress.)

ON THE COVER: The Friends Academy, located on East Main Street at the head of Chester Avenue, was built in 1785 on land purchased by the Friends Meeting from Ephraim Haines. The one-room, stone schoolhouse faced away from Main Street to overlook the valley. One of the original stone walls is visible on the right rear of this photograph, which shows the academy and its students in 1889. (Courtesy of Moorestown Friends School.)

IMAGES
of America

MOORESTOWN

Kimberly L. Bunn and Lynne F. Schill
with the Moorestown Improvement Association

ARCADIA
PUBLISHING

Published by Arcadia Publishing
Charleston, South Carolina

Library of Congress Control Number: 2014933313

For all general information, please contact Arcadia Publishing:
Telephone 843-853-2070
Fax 843-853-0044
E-mail sales@arcadiapublishing.com
For customer service and orders:
Toll-Free 1-888-313-2665

Visit us on the Internet at www.arcadiapublishing.com

In 1740, Henry Warrington planted the buttonwood tree at the southwest corner of the Friends cemetery for use as a hitching post. It became a bulletin board where important notices were attached. The sign on the left in this c. 1890 photograph reads, "The British Army passed under these trees after evacuating Philadelphia June 1778." (Courtesy of Moorestown Improvement Association [MIA].)

CONTENTS

ACKNOWLEDGMENTS

First and foremost, the authors would like to thank the Historical Society of Moorestown and its tireless pursuit of the town's history. This book would not have been possible without the help of Bill Archer, Stephanie Herz, and Lenny Wagner of the society and their generous willingness to share time, photographs, and knowledge. Unless otherwise credited, the images included here were provided by the Historical Society of Moorestown.

We would also like to thank the Moorestown Friends School, which offered unlimited access to its library of photographs and history. We must also thank Bill Newborg at the Moorestown Community House, the fire departments, the churches, the wonderful staff of the Moorestown Library, and the numerous businesses and individuals who offered information and photographs. We cannot express enough our gratitude to our husbands, Matthew Bunn, for looking after hearth and home, and David Schill, for the hours of scanning. We would be remiss if we did not acknowledge the past officers of the Moorestown Improvement Association who provided a vast amount of knowledge through detailed meeting minutes that are the basis for much of the book. Finally, we would like to offer our appreciation for the literary works of James C. Purdy and George DeCou, whose detailed, and sometimes baffling, accounts of early life in Moorestown were indispensable. Any discrepancies are due to the challenges of piecing together many conflicting stories and clues from the past.

We dedicate this book to all those individuals and organizations, past and present, who have worked to preserve the history and heritage of Moorestown.

INTRODUCTION

The Lenni Lenape, who called themselves the "Original People," lived in bark houses called wigwams and traveled with the seasons between what we now know as Pennsylvania, New Jersey, and Delaware. They were the first residents of what is now Moorestown, with evidence of camps at Swedes Run near the Rancocas Creek and along the Pennsauken Creek and near Indian Springs on the Ridge, the high point of the area along which Main Street now runs. Densely forested with an ample supply of freshwater, this was undoubtedly a beautiful setting in which to live.

The earliest landowner of record was William Biddle, who received his portion of land from William Penn in 1677. Of this share of land, he sold a portion on Rancocas Creek in 1686 to Thomas Rodman of Rhode Island and another section along the Ridge to the west to Thomas's brother John Rodman. There is no record that these men ever settled here.

On September 25, 1681, the West Jersey Assembly authorized the building of a road that would connect the English settlements at Burlington in the north and Salem in the south. The work of clearing the road began in 1682 along what were mostly American Indian trails that were invariably the easiest paths, including one along the Ridge that probably went between the native camps. It was called both the Kings Highway and Old Salem Road. It ran through what was to become Haddonfield and Moorestown and then crossed the Rancocas Creek at Hollinsheads Ferry.

In 1682, John and Sarah Roberts, William and Mary Matlack, and Timothy and Rachael Hancock were the first English settlers to arrive on the shore of the north branch of the Pennsauken Creek. There, so the story goes, they lived in caves or dugouts along the side of the hills until logs could be felled and small homes built. Each of these families had secured portions of the land in what was then West Jersey before they left England. They built homesteads on large fertile tracts. John Rudderow, William Clarke, Robert Stiles, and Thomas French quickly followed. Around the same time, John Borton, John Hollinshead, and the Hooten family built homesteads on the banks of the Rancocas Creek and began farming the land.

By the early 1700s, the area was known as Chester Township. It was a vast collection of farms spread throughout the area between the Rancocas and Pennsauken Creeks and from the Delaware River into the edges of what we know as Mount Laurel and Cherry Hill. The early settlers were members of the Religious Society of Friends, also known as Quakers, who gathered in homes for worship until the first Friends Meeting was erected and schools were built. Businesses followed, and soon there were tanneries, blacksmith shops, and, of course, taverns. These gathered along the Ridge, close to an easy supply of freshwater at the Indian Springs, and gradually became a village.

In 1742, Thomas Moore opened a tavern on the west end of the village. Moore began buying and selling tracts of land, becoming what may have been our first real estate agent. The village is referred to on some early maps as Moorfield or Mooresfield and the Pennsauken Creek as Moor's Creek. The village became officially known as Moorestown in 1802, when the first post office was opened.

As the years passed, villages sprang up throughout Chester Township, including Westtown, New Albany, Fairview, Bridgeboro, Palmyra, Rivertown, Colestown, Centerton, Maple Shade, Stanwick, and North Bend. A border change with Evesham Township gave us our present eastern border. In 1860, Cinnaminson broke off, taking the villages to the west within its borders. The village of Moorestown officially withdrew from Chester Township in 1922 and became the Township of Moorestown. The last vestige of the original Chester Township officially changed its name to Maple Shade in 1948.

Moorestown had innovative thinkers, acres of fertile land, and the perfect placement along Kings Highway, which added to its growth. It soon became known for exceptional peaches, apples, hybrid berries, asparagus, and other produce, which was taken to the markets of Philadelphia and New York City. These goods were so desired that nurseries sprang up to sell plants, seeds, and exotic specimen plants, some of which went to the estates and large parks along the East Coast. The railroad brought industry and prominent executives from Camden and Philadelphia who built large estates.

Through all the growth, Moorestown has changed in many ways. Much of the farmland is gone, housing developments have sprung up, and traffic congestion and parking issues are small irritants of daily life. Yet, it has in many ways stayed true to its roots. Farmland and open space are being preserved, churches are flourishing, schools are still excellent, the oldest part of downtown has been placed in the National Register of Historic Places, and the residential neighborhoods remain desirable places for families to grow.

Shown here is an advertising page from the May 1904 Moorestown Improvement Association monthly newspaper.

One

SETTLEMENT

The first Quaker meetinghouse was built on the northwest corner of what is now Main Street and Chester Avenue. The small log structure burned down in 1720 and was replaced with a larger stone building. This was demolished in 1802 when the current brick meetinghouse was built across Main Street. In 1827, two factions developed within the Meeting, and the Orthodox faction built this wood structure, shown in this c. 1880 image, on the west end of the property. It was removed in 1897 and replaced with a larger brick structure.

The distillery, pictured here around 1900, was located near the Hollinshead farm on the east end of old Kings Highway and was one of several distilleries built in early Moorestown. In 1915, the local chapter of the Women's Christian Temperance Union succeeded in its effort to have alcohol banned in Moorestown.

Built in the early 1870s as tenant housing for factory and mill workers and their families, the twin house shown here was located at 154 East Main Street. Several of these homes lined the south side of East Main Street at the time. At 140 East Main Street, there was a long, low house that was split into tenements for workers where a colorful episode took place. The tenants of the house were known for brawling and disorder. The local gossip says that a vigilance committee of townspeople was formed in 1830, and the tenants were told to move on. One night shortly after, the house was razed with ropes and chains.

Built in 1721, the Zelley House located on North Stanwick Road is one of the oldest remaining homes in Moorestown. It stands within the borders of 500 acres purchased by Thomas Rodman in 1686. Although they did not live here until decades after it was built, many generations of the Zelley family were born and raised in the home.

The Matlack farm, first deeded in 1695, comprised 100 acres along the south branch of the Pennsauken Creek, which is now the dividing line between Moorestown and Maple Shade but was originally all in Chester Township. The farm's blacksmith shop shown in this c. 1930 photograph was built in 1786 on what now is Lenola Road. The Matlack mill was located near what is now Pleasant Valley Avenue. (Courtesy of Library of Congress.)

John Cox purchased a plot of land on the north side of Main Street across from the Friends Meeting in 1745 and built his tavern, shown here around 1880. Early town meetings were held in the tavern until Old Town Hall was built on Main Street in 1812. The first stagecoach line, founded in 1759, stopped at Moore's Tavern on the west end of the village and Cox's Tavern on the east. The tavern was demolished in 1904 to make space for a lawn for the Doughten homestead, partially seen on the left.

The West End Hotel, pictured around 1885, was originally named the Washington Hotel. It stood on the northeast corner of Main Street and North Washington Avenue and was the headquarters of William Doughten's stagecoach line, begun in 1831. An 1896 map shows the West End Hotel containing a bar and a billiard hall. North Washington at Main Street gradually narrowed as the hotel built barns for horses and carriages, and it eventually disappeared altogether.

The house located at 512 Camden Avenue, shown in this c. 1900 image, is one of the oldest in town. The earliest section of the house, a one-room structure, was built in 1700 by Thomas French Jr., a prominent citizen of the time. It was reportedly raided for provisions by both sides during the Revolutionary War. The property stayed in the family until 1837, when it was purchased by Elwood Hollinshead; it remained in the Hollinshead family until 1965. It is listed in the National Register of Historic Places.

Built about 1800 as a tavern and originally known as the William Penn Hotel, the Coles Hotel, shown in this c. 1880 image, stood at the northwest corner of Main Street and Chester Avenue, just west of the Friends cemetery. It was an early stagecoach stop on the east end of town. It was demolished to make way for the current bank building in 1926.

Pictured around 1923, this house was built by Thomas and Mary Cowperthwaite in 1742, and it still stands on the northwest corner of Kings Highway and Lenola Road. The Cowperthwaite farm was surveyed in 1684 and included land in both Moorestown and Maple Shade, which was then

John and Grace Hollinshead purchased 550 acres on the Rancocas Creek in 1678. Pictured around 1890, the house on Centerton Road was built in 1767 and is now known as the Thomas Tallman House. It was rumored to have been used as a hiding place on the Underground Railroad. The Hollinsheads were Quaker abolitionists who operated the ferry that continued the Old Salem Road across the Rancocas. On the far side of the creek was Timbuctoo, a haven for fugitive slaves who lived in the dense woods near Mount Holly.

all Chester Township. The sign reads "Barlow & Co." and lists lots for sale in "Lenola Heights" from $50 to $400. Thomas Barlow built many bungalows throughout the area. (Courtesy of Maple Shade Historical Society.)

Built in 1767 along with the main house, the Tallman smokehouse, shown in this c. 1935 photograph, still stands on Centerton Road. In the autumn, hogs and turkeys were butchered, heavily salted, and hung in the smokehouse. A smoldering, long-burning fire was maintained to slowly preserve the meat. This process took up to two weeks and provided meat for the winter when no other means of preservation was available. (Courtesy of Library of Congress.)

Shown in the c. 1880 image above, the oldest portion of the Smith Cadbury mansion was part of a 160-acre property purchased by Joshua Humphries in 1738. In 1766, the house was sold to Samuel Smith, whose family resided there until 1798. The British army stopped overnight in Moorestown in June 1778 following its retreat from Philadelphia. The Hessian officer in command of the army, General Knyphausen, made himself at home here. The mansion, which still stands at 12 High Street, is home to the Historical Society of Moorestown and is listed in the National Register of Historic Places. The family cemetery, shown in the c. 1880 photograph at left, was on the Charles Haines farm, located on the north branch of the Pennsauken Creek just south of Camden Avenue.

Two

VILLAGE

The common scene in this view of Main Street looking east from Chester Avenue shows much about the tranquility of everyday life in the village during its early years. The Doughten Dry Goods Store and homestead at the corner is on the left, next to Cox's Tavern. The store carried not only dry staples, but also seeds, coal, wood, and farming implements. The bridged swale, on the right was common on dirt roads for water runoff. (Courtesy of MIA.)

The view in this c. 1895 photograph of the Matlack house and barn speaks to the agrarian roots of Moorestown. Initially, all the land in the village was farmland. As the village grew along the Ridge and tradesmen arrived to service the farms with materials and tools, the farms grew larger to meet increased demand.

The original J.S. Collins hardware and feed store on Mill Street, which eventually grew into a chain of five stores at train stops along the Camden & Amboy line, is shown in this c. 1875 image. John S. Collins eventually purchased acres of land in South Florida, where he formed the Miami Beach Development in 1911—the first use of that name.

The Crider farm was located at what is now the junction of Lenola and New Albany Roads. The farm's goods were transported to the local groceries in the delivery wagon shown here around 1880. The Frech wagon works, located on the far west end of Chester Township, developed a unique "cut-under truck shelving" system for transporting produce. (Courtesy of MIA.)

Frank Garrigues's Cash Grocery, shown in this c. 1890 photograph, was located on what is now Third Street at Chester Avenue. The store sold both local items and luxury wares like pulled figs, California celery, and Neufchâtel cheese. Garrigues also had a mail-order system and home delivery. (Courtesy of Moorestown Community House.)

Moorestown's first post office opened in 1802 with Isaac Wilkins as postmaster. As the postmasters were local business owners, the post office moved to each new postmaster's place of business. From 1819 to 1839, Gilbert Page ran the post office from his store and residence, located in what is now Roberts Hall on the Friends School property at 86 East Main Street, seen above in 1929. Pages Lane, which runs adjacent to Roberts Hall, is named in Page's honor. Albert L. Brock, pictured at left, was named postmaster in 1896, when the post office was in the Old Masonic Hall at 61 East Main Street.

The frame portion of the Elisha Barcklow House at 274 West Main Street, shown in this c. 1890 photograph, was built in 1765. At the rear of the property is the spring that supplied the local American Indian tribes and the earliest settlers with fresh, cool water. Local oral tradition states that this was a stop on the Underground Railroad. There is an odd vaulted compartment in the basement that shows evidence of an exterior tunnel that ran to the rear barn, which would have been a good means of escape. Elisha's son J. Harry owned the Barcklow Meat Market and the slaughterhouse on the property, shown in the c. 1900 image below. The slaughterhouse, which stood in the rear of the property, was used by the town butchers: Mortlands, Tippenhauers, and A.W. Deacon. Butchering was done on Tuesday and Fridays.

John O'Donnell opened his blacksmith and wagon works shop at 115–121 South Church Street in 1905. By 1911, the building had been moved around the corner to Prospect Avenue. It was demolished for the construction of Our Lady of Good Counsel School in the 1960s.

Ice was harvested in large chunks from the local frozen creeks, dragged by sled to an icehouse, and packed with straw or sawdust for insulation. Packed securely, the ice would last until the following winter. During warm months, icemen delivered chunk ice to homes and businesses using the type of wagon shown in this c. 1880 photograph. (Courtesy of MIA.)

The front portion of Old Town Hall, then known as the Town House, was built in 1812 at 40 East Main Street. A rear addition was built in 1859, and a jail was added in 1876. The Town House was the center of activity for the area, hosting civic groups, political meetings, lectures, suppers, and the earliest silent movie showings. It continued as township offices until the new town hall was built in 1971.

The Joshua Bispham House, located at 139 East Main Street and the corner of Schooley Street, was built in 1735. The house, shown in the center of this c. 1900 photograph, was used to house junior officers of the Hessian army following its retreat from Philadelphia in June 1778. The house to the right was built in 1720 and was at one time used as a tannery.

A steam tractor on Chester Avenue carries water pipes for E.C. Worrell Plumbing, whose office can be seen behind the tractor. The Moorestown Improvement Association initiated the purchase of the water system from its private shareholders following the typhoid epidemic of early 1912. Prior to the acquisition, water was sampled from the local water system and found to be polluted. The Moorestown Camden Turnpike Company was chartered in 1849 to improve the damage to Main Street caused by heavy wagon traffic. Shares were sold and tollbooths were set up to pay for timely repairs, as seen below on East Main Street.

The funeral home at 78 East Main Street is the longest-operating business in Moorestown. Cabinetmaker Samuel Jones bought the house in 1843 and began the undertaking business on the west side of the home. Jones died in 1885, and the business was sold to Henry Rambo. After subsequent owners, Douglas Lewis bought the building and business in 1964. It is now owned by John Engelman, who has retained the Lewis Funeral Home name. Elwood C. and John C. Belton owned the Belton Funeral Home on West Main Street in the early 1900s. Below is their funeral carriage in front of Elwood's West Second Street home. They later moved the business to 334 Chester Avenue.

Hugh Hollinshead was born in 1753 to a clock-making family in Burlington. He moved to Moorestown, where he lived and kept a shop at 260 East Main Street. The house, shown here in the early 1900s, was built in 1770. His cousin Morgan also maintained a clock business in Moorestown.

William G. LeConey was born into an old and long-established Moorestown family in 1868. His father, William, owned a construction company that built many of the finest homes in town as well as the First Baptist Church on Main Street. William, the son, learned carpentry but settled into the business of selling real estate and insurance. He is shown in this c. 1930 photograph in front of his shop at 27 West Main Street, now the home of Carl's Shoes.

Three

TOWN

MOORESTOWN COMMUNITY HOUSE
Opening Week Program
Moorestown, New Jersey, April 11-16, 1926

An unnamed benefactor offered $100,000 to the town for the building of a community center if the town would rally to raise an additional $50,000 by June 1, 1924. It was to be a center for charitable and philanthropic activities in the town. The Moorestown Community House was dedicated on April 11, 1926. It was later revealed that Eldridge Reeves Johnson of the Victor Talking Machine Company was the benefactor. (Courtesy of Moorestown Community House.)

The Dyer Livery was located on Plum Street off of Second Street prior to 1900. At that time, S.J. Zelley's Livery was located behind the Coles Hotel at Chester and Main Streets and moved to the Plum Street location, shown above in 1905. It remained there until at least 1917. The Grange Hall, shown below in 1910, was built in 1886 and was the location of one of the most progressive Granges in Burlington County. Granges throughout the country became politically active in the 1890s.

"FORKS OF ROAD," MOORESTOWN, N. J.

Tell Emma I will write that letter sooner then

The trolley system began in 1901 with the extension of the Camden & Suburban line to Moorestown. The Burlington County Traction Company opened its line from Borton Landing Road to Mount Holly in May 1904. The two lines merged to become the Public Service Company. Trolley service was discontinued in 1928 with the advent of buses. The Camden & Amboy Railroad came through Moorestown in 1867. This brought fast and easy access to the city of Camden for both passengers and freight and was the beginning of an influx of businessmen and their families, as well as more mechanized industry.

The Rodman Building, shown above in 1914, was constructed at 84 East Main Street in 1900. It was the home of the Moorestown National Bank Company and the Burlington County Savings Deposit Trust Company (BCSDT). The structure was demolished in 1965 to make way for a more modern office building. In 1926, the two banks went their separate ways. Shown below is the laying of the cornerstone for the newly named Moorestown Trust Company at 41 East Main Street. The BCSDT, later known as the Burlington County Trust Company, built its new home at 101 East Main Street that same year.

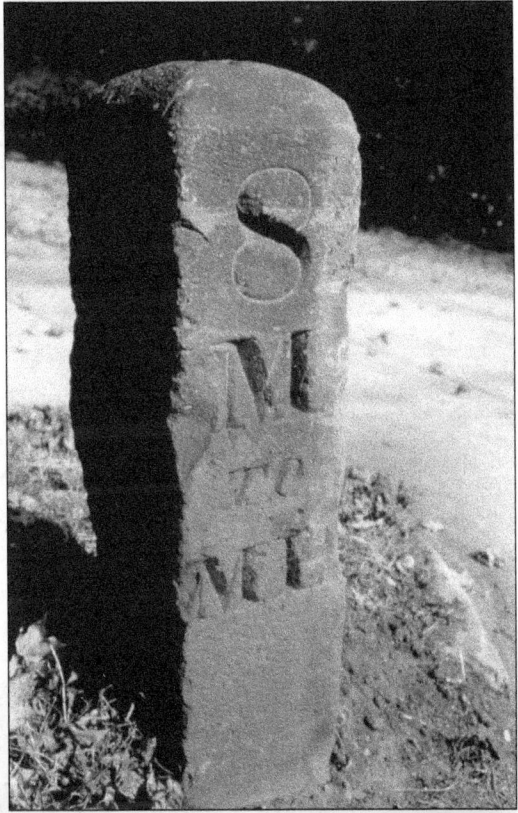

In 1844, the residents of Chester Township met to form the Moorestown-Camden Turnpike, with tollgates at Lenola Road and Forks of the Road (where Camden Avenue and Main Street meet) and at Marter Avenue. By 1849, the turnpike stretched from Mount Holly to Camden. Pictured at right is the mile marker still located at the head of Moorestown-Mount Laurel Road on Main Street, showing 8 miles to Mount Holly. The Moorestown fairgrounds, shown below around 1900, once occupied the seven acres northeast of the railroad on North Stanwick Road. The grounds were used for exhibitions of horses, cattle, other livestock, and farm products. Organized by the Moorestown Agricultural and Industrial Society, the fairs were held twice per year, and in 1886, the Stanwick Railroad Station was built to accommodate the fairs. Stanwick Road was originally called Fairground Avenue.

The *Moorestown Chronicle* was first published on December 10, 1878, announcing that it would be a weekly paper of independent politics. The proprietor was J.E. Watkins, a longtime resident, who brought W.J. Lovell, a printer from Philadelphia, to manage the business. In a year, the company name was changed to Watkins and Lovell, and on June 18, 1883, Watkins retired and William Lovell became the sole proprietor. In August 1885, the *Chronicle* moved into its new permanent home on Chester Avenue, shown above in 1938. Big changes came to Moorestown as the population and congestion grew. The c. 1900 image below shows the laying of Belgian blocks to support the new trolley tracks on Main Street.

Pictured in 1912, the home of Dr. Nathan Thorne was located at 77 East Main Street. There is no record of when it was demolished, but the one-story building that now stands at this location, last used as a paint store, was built in 1923. The residence shown below, built in the early 1800s, was demolished to make way for the building of the Acme Supermarket on Chester Avenue. The Acme was built in 1955 to reflect the general design of the Friends Meeting House.

Pennsylvania Railroad Station, Moorestown, N.J.

Above is a postcard view of Chester Avenue Station on the Camden & Amboy Railroad, which was laid in 1867. The coming of the railroad brought wealthy businessmen from Camden and Philadelphia whose families wanted more rural surroundings. At its peak in 1900, there were more that 20 passenger and freight trains per day. In the late 1800s, a group of 10 businessmen formed the Moorestown Land Company and bought 55 acres north of the railroad, and each built a fine and substantial home in the area. Gradually, the other lots were filled. These men were called "crows," the first commuters to the city for the workday who "flew" home at night. Below is a c. 1900 view of East Oak Avenue during development.

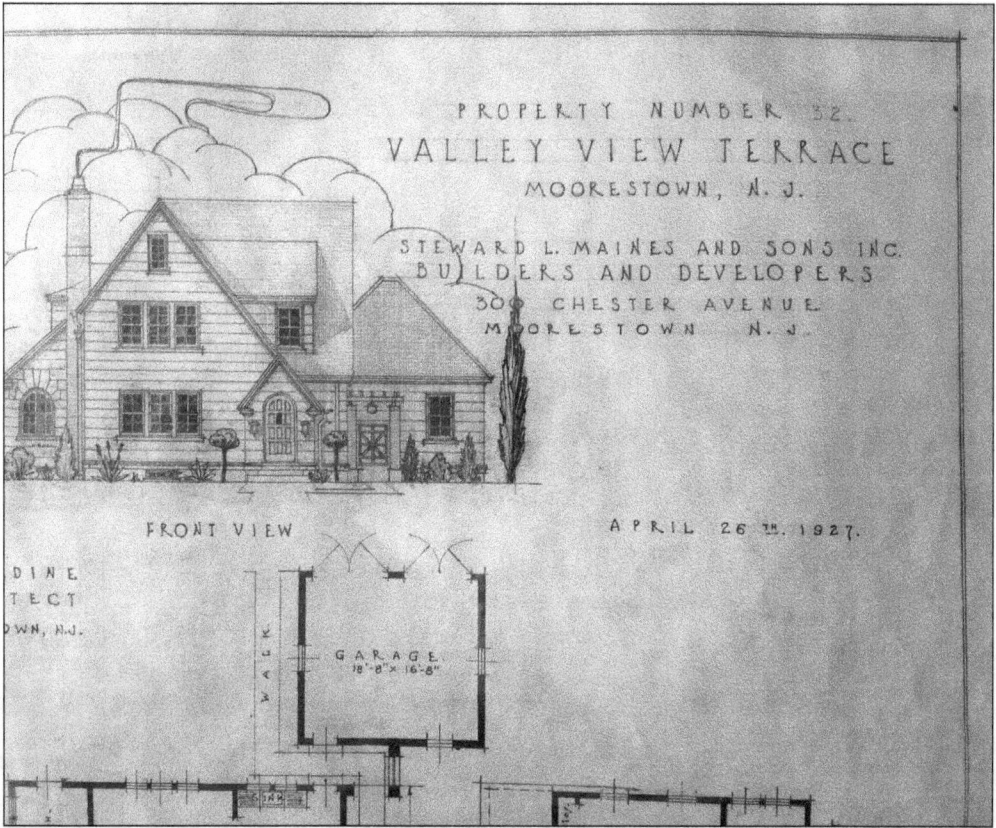

The Pleasant Valley section of town, just west of Pleasant Valley Avenue, was developed in the 1920s by local builder Steward Maines and local architect W.H. Kenderdine. On Valley View Terrace and Lakeview Terrace, 20 homes were built, most with rear alleys for parking and trash removal. Above is the architect's rendering of one of the houses. Below is a photograph of a Valley View home taken in the mid-1970s. Valley View Terrace remains a cul-de-sac, while Lakeview Terrace has been opened through to Stratford Terrace, but hints of the cul-de-sac remain. (Both, courtesy of MIA.)

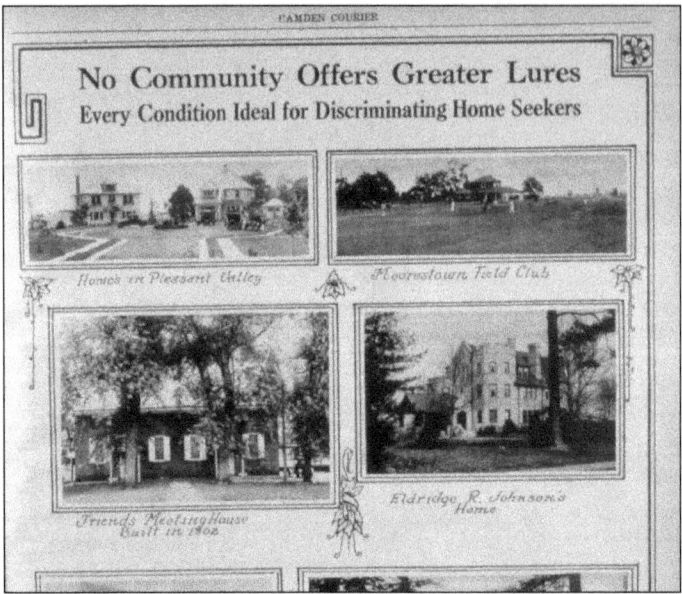

This advertisement was placed in the *Camden Courier* in the late 1920s to extol the lovely virtues of Moorestown as a wonderful place to live and raise a family. Shown clockwise from upper left are two homes in Pleasant Valley, the Moorestown Field Club, Eldridge R. Johnson's palatial estate, and the 1802 Friends Meeting House. (Courtesy of MIA.)

During the 1920s, Moorestown grew at a rapid pace. Thomas Barlow and Company built small bungalows throughout the town. One could buy six rooms and a bath for $4,500. This photograph shows Barlow bungalows on Fairview Avenue. The stock market crash of 1929 ended the building boom. (Courtesy of MIA.)

Four

CHURCHES

The first Friends Meeting House was a log cabin built in 1700 on the northwest corner of Chester Avenue where the current cemetery is located. This burned down in 1720 and was replaced with a larger stone building. By 1800, the building was no longer adequate, so the brick building that still stands across Main Street from the cemetery was constructed in 1802. It is shown here in 1890. (Courtesy of Moorestown Community House.)

A doctrinal split of the Friends Meeting members occurred in 1827, and the Orthodox branch built a separate meeting at the west end of the property, shown above around 1900. They merged again in 1951. This is now the West Building of the Friends School, and it houses the lower school gym and has other school uses. The Greenleaf, shown in the c. 1965 photograph below, was built in 1820 by Charles French and purchased by Edward Harris Jr. in 1845. By 1917, it was officially a home for the aged run by the Friends and continued as such until it was recently acquired by the Moorestown Friends School, where it is in use as classrooms. (Above, courtesy of Moorestown Friends School; below, courtesy of MIA.)

The original Trinity Episcopal Church of Moorestown, shown above, was built in 1837 at the corner of Main and Church Streets. Edward Harris donated the land for the original church and brought the bell from England for its tower. In 1929, all but the chapel was demolished and rebuilt in the English Gothic style with church, rectory, and cloister. Eldridge Johnson donated $324,000 for the renovations. Below, the centerpiece of the Evergreens Retirement Home on Bridgeboro Road was built in the early 1920s as a Johnson family home. The retirement home moved there in 1949 and has since grown to include assisted-living and long-term care. It continues to be run by the Episcopal Church.

Episcopal Home, Moorestown, N. J.

The First Baptist Church began meeting in the home of Edward Harris in 1810. By 1835, the services were held in Old Town Hall. In 1837, the congregants decided to build their own house of worship. During the construction, the carpenter shop was destroyed by fire, but the building continued. The members dug the basement themselves, and the finished building was dedicated on August 10, 1838. Shown above in the late 1880s are the Main Street church and parsonage. The Second Baptist Church was organized in 1893 under Reverend Wooden. Members met in homes and Old Town Hall until the Moorestown Friends donated an old frame structure and it was moved to Mill Street. The photograph below shows the expanded church in 1911.

In 1802, Bishop Asbury came to Moorestown and held a Methodist meeting at the home of Hugh Hollinshead. The group later met at Old Town Hall until Edward Harris gave the members land on the south side of Main Street. They erected a plain brick building without a bell tower or spire. In 1860, they built a brick structure on the north side of Main Street, shown at right around 1890. In 1901, the stone front was added, as shown below. In 1957, they purchased a large lot at Camden and Pleasant Valley Avenues and built a modern fellowship hall, where they worshipped until the sanctuary was built in 1967. The modern structures were designed by noted architect Malcolm Wells. (Both, courtesy of First United Methodist Church of Moorestown.)

CHURCH OF OUR LADY OF GOOD COUNSEL
MOORESTOWN, NEW JERSEY

When negotiating for property on which to build the first Roman Catholic church in Moorestown, the pastor enlisted the help of a friend, as many people in the area were reluctant to sell land to Catholics. When asked by the seller, William Haines, what type of factory would be built on the land, it is said that the response was "a factory for repairing souls." As there was no shoemaker in town, Haines went through with the transaction. The original church was completed in 1870 and was named the Church of Our Lady and St. Patrick. After storm damage, a larger English Gothic–style church was built and was renamed Church of Our Lady of Good Counsel (OLGC), which was completed in 1896. The two-story building shown below was the original rectory purchased from Edward Harris in 1905. (Both, courtesy of OLGC.)

Good Counsel Rectory,
Moorestown, N. J.

GOOD COUNSEL RECTORY

The wood-frame rectory of OLGC was demolished
in 1913 and replaced with the present stone
rectory, built by J.S. Rogers of Moorestown in
the Queen Anne Tudor style. The stone of
the building matches that of the main church.
(Courtesy of OLGC.)

The cornerstone of the original Bethel AME
Church, shown at right in 1935, was laid in 1884.
The congregation first met in homes and in Van
Sciver's Hall on West Main Street until property
could be purchased on North Church Street. The
simple wooden structure, with a cupola, held 200
worshipers and was destroyed by fire. The current,
larger building was erected to replace it.

First Presbyterian Church, Moorestown, N. J.

Presbyterian gatherings were originally held at the Thomas S. Collings home at 245 East Main Street and then at the Grange Hall on East Main Street. In 1887, the members began raising funds for a church building. They then met in Heulings Hall on Chester Avenue and officially organized as a church. In 1891, the cornerstone was laid for the original First Presbyterian Church at 318 Chester Avenue, pictured here, and the church opened for worship in 1892.

The cornerstone of the new First Presbyterian Church was laid in 1955 on property donated to the church by J.S. Collins. Services began in the new church at the corner of Chester Avenue and Bridgeboro Road in 1956. In 1956, the church sold the old property and building on Chester Avenue to the Lutherans.

The former home of Eldridge Johnson at 255 East Main Street was purchased in 1946 by the Evangelical Lutheran Church in America for use as a skilled-nursing facility, shown above in the mid-1900s. Sunday services of the Moorestown Lutherans were begun at that time in the Lutheran Home and then in the Moorestown Community House while finalizing the purchase of the old Presbyterian church on Chester Avenue in 1950. They renamed the parish St. Matthew Evangelical Lutheran Church. In 1962, they built the rear education building. The final service, shown below in June 1971, was held in the Chester Avenue sanctuary prior to its demolition. In 1972, they dedicated the new building, which remains today. The new structure was designed by local architect Herman Hassinger, a member of the church. (Both, courtesy of St. Matthew Lutheran Church.)

The Methodist Protestant Church split with the Methodist Episcopal body in March 1883 for doctrinal reasons and formed its own church. Meetings were held temporarily in Old Town Hall. A lot was purchased on the north side of Main Street just east of Union Street from the estate of George Heaton, where there was a blacksmith and wheelwright shop. Building began in 1883, and it opened for services in 1884. It is pictured above in the 1960s. The spire of the 1884 church building held the only town clock. The structure was demolished in 1969 and rebuilt as the Moorestown Bible Church. The First Church of Christ, Scientist, shown below, is located at the southeast corner of Kings Highway and Pleasant Valley Avenue. The building was constructed in the 1920s as the sales office for the Pleasant Valley development.

Five

SCHOOLS

The ground for the Chester Brick School, one of the original schools in Chester Township, was purchased from Job and Ann Cowperthwaite, and the schoolhouse was built in 1785 by the Chester Preparative Meeting of Friends. The school was located on Kings Highway west of Lenola Road on what came to be known as School House Lane. In 1827, the Hicksite Friends took over the school and maintained it until 1872, when the county acquired it as a public school. The school closed in 1917 and was sold to Joseph Matlack, who used it to house blueberry pickers during the summer months. It was later destroyed by fire.

Anne Lees Clement, pictured around 1880, taught at the Chester Brick School in 1876 after the Hicksite Friends took over the school. The Moorestown Friends faculty and school committee is shown below outside of the Friends High School on Chester Avenue in 1886. Although some of the names are obscured, several old Moorestown families are represented, including J. Lippincott (center rear), M. Lippincott (front row, third from the right) and members of the Wilson, Willets, and Rogers families. It is interesting to note the beards on the men and the very dark, unornamented style that prevailed in the Friends Society at the time. (Both, courtesy of Moorestown Friends School.)

Moorestown Friends H.S
School Committee + Faculty
1886

The Moorestown Friends Academy offered a full range of classes in the fields of math, history, geography, science, and languages, both English and foreign. Pictured above around 1915 is the sewing class taught by Grace Benedict, standing at center rear. Seen below near the remaining stone wall from the original 1785 one-room school built on the site is a lower school class from the early 1900s. Teacher Marion Wood is seated in the center of the children. Margaret DeCou is second from left in the middle row, and her younger sister Elizabeth is in the middle row, far right. (Both, courtesy of Moorestown Friends School.)

In 1829, the Hicksite Friends built a wood-frame schoolhouse known as the Friends High School on Chester Avenue near what is now Second Street. In 1880, a larger brick structure was built at the corner of Chester Avenue and Second Street, shown above around 1880. In 1883, while already serving 12 grade levels, it expanded and began to include the first kindergarten class in Moorestown. In 1891, Alice Paul was one of eleven students in the kindergarten class. The photograph below shows the expanded school in 1900. In 1920, the two factions of the Friends reconciled, and the high school met at the Chester Avenue location and lower grades at the Main Street site. (Both, courtesy of Moorestown Friends School.)

In 1926, the new headmaster of the combined Friends School switched the location of the schools, moving the high school to the Main Street campus. This allowed for larger expansions of the school and its grounds. The above 1929 image shows the raised wooden tennis court, where games and physical education courses were held. That year, all grades were moved to the main campus. The Chester Avenue building was demolished in 1935 to make ways for the new post office. Below is a 1950s view of the elementary school building after multiple additions to the original 1785 stone school building. It was demolished in 1965 after the new elementary school was completed. (Both, courtesy of Moorestown Friends School.)

Pictured at left is Mary Lippincott, who ran a boarding school for young ladies in her home from 1843 to 1883. Mary was the second wife of Isaac Lippincott, who farmed the area east of Stanwick Road. Their house sat at what is now 435 East Main Street, shown below in this c. 1880 image. Mary was a refined Quaker lady who was a noted educator of her day. When Isaac retired from farming, they added a wing to the house and the third floor for student rooms, and Mary opened her school. The school was patronized by some of the most cultured families in South Jersey and Philadelphia. Manners and deportment were taught along with the usual subjects. The house became a hotel in 1890 and was demolished in 1919.

In the 1800s, private schools proliferated in Moorestown. The Moorestown Private School and Kraus' Kindergarten, shown above in 1891, was located on East Central Avenue and used teaching methods based on Quaker philosophies. Rachel Rogers was the principal. Children entered by the age of three so they could be well prepared for their subsequent educations. Shown in the c. 1900 image below, the Men's Seminary, a boarding school, was located on the northwest corner of East Main and Schooley Streets. The Weld School was conducted by Rev. H Hastings Weld at the rectory of Trinity Episcopal Church from 1854 to 1870. (Above, courtesy of Moorestown Friends School.)

The first public school in Moorestown village was this small frame structure that stood on the southeast corner of Church and Second Streets. Built in 1835, it was called the Friendship School and is pictured at left around 1870. It was moved across Second Street to the northeast corner in 1850. A very small fee was levied per day for attendance because New Jersey did not establish a free public-school system until 1871. The school was sold and moved back across Second Street in 1873, and the larger free public school, shown below around 1880, was built in its place. A larger brick and stone school was later built on the site of what is now the new town hall on Second Street.

The brick school at the corner of North Lenola and New Albany Roads, shown above in this c. 1900 image, was built in the very late 1800s after the public school system was instituted in the state. It is presently owned by the Christadelphian Ecclesia and used as a place of worship. The frame building pictured in the c. 1900 image below was on the Old Salem Road east of Westfield Road. It is known both as Pages School and Poplar Grove School.

No. 7 School was built on the west side of North Church Street in the latter part of the 1800s. Built to educate the children who lived in and around North Church Street, the school was eventually demolished. Shown above is a c. 1930 class picture from No. 7 School. Pictured below in 1912 is an old horse-drawn school bus on Second Street in front of No. 9 School. (Both, courtesy of Moorestown Community House.)

Public High School, Moorestown, N. J.

A new Moorestown High School building, known as No. 9 School, was built on Second Street between Church Street and North Washington Avenue. The cornerstone was laid in 1906. By 1914, it was in use as an elementary school and a larger high school was constructed on North Church Street. Below is the Moorestown High School graduating class of 1921. The question arises as to whether there was there a uniform or whether the sailor shirt and tie was the style that year.

Moorestown High School was built on the southeast corner of Church and Second Streets in 1914 to accommodate the needs of a growing town. The north-end addition containing the gymnasium and cafeteria was added in 1934. The house shown below was removed for the gym addition. The 1914 building was demolished in 1971 for construction of the municipal complex, but the later gym addition still stands at the corner of Church and Third Streets.

Shown above in 1926 is the laying of the cornerstone of the Religious Education Building of Our Lady of Good Counsel Church. It was built behind the existing church and is shown in this view looking from Prospect Avenue toward the rear of the church building, which was constructed in 1896. A later addition to the school was completed in 1962, shown below, when O'Donnell's Wagon Works on Prospect Avenue near Church Street was demolished. (Both, courtesy of OLGC.)

THE SISTERS WHO TEACH OUR YOUTH

Standing: (left to right) Sisters Rita Francine, Mary Carmel, Rita David and Joseph Bernadette.
Seated: Sister Saint Mary, Mother Ethel De Sales, Sisters Marie Ursula and Joan Amelia.

The Our Lady of Good Counsel School was opened in 1927 with classes for first through eighth grades. Nuns from the Congregation of the Sisters of St. Joseph, shown above in 1960, came to teach the classes. In 1928, the church built an addition to the structure on Main Street east of the church as a convent for the sisters. In 1986, the convent was turned into the early childhood center for the parish. Below is a 1934 photograph of the eighth-grade graduating class of Our Lady of Good Counsel School. (Both, courtesy of OLGC.)

Six

BUSINESS AND INDUSTRY

J.S. Collins Company, pictured around 1900, was the largest hardware and building supply business in the area. By the 1950s, there was a Collins store at five stops along the Camden & Amboy Railroad. Eventually, the main J.S. Collins Company in Moorestown had the railroad install a siding off of the main line for deliveries. In the early 1900s, the company expanded to both sides of Mill Street, which included an ice manufacturer and cold-storage plant that ran day and night, as well as a planing mill for lumber. (Courtesy of Moorestown Hardware.)

Johnson & Stokes'

Garden and Flower Seeds

Can be obtained at

FLORACROFT

GARDEN GREENHOUSES

Cor. Oak and Chester Aves.

MOORESTOWN, N. J.

VEGETABLE PLANTS IN SEASON

Walter P. Stokes joined the Philadelphia Seed Company, owned by Herbert W. Johnson of Merchantville, and it was renamed the Johnson & Stokes Seed Company in 1881. As shown in the advertisement at left from the May 1905 Moorestown Improvement Association newsletter, seeds and bulbs were sold locally from its Floracroft Greenhouses at the corner of Chester and Oak Avenues. The highly successful enterprise was dissolved in 1906, and Walter Stokes resumed operating under his previous business name, Stokes' Standard Seeds, and then as Stokes Seed Company. (Courtesy of MIA.)

Stokes Seeds grew bedding plants for sale on Lippincott Avenue between Oak and Maple Avenues, shown here around 1894. By 1910, the company had built multiple greenhouses on the site as well as on its Flynn Avenue property. In 1926, the company's property on Flynn Avenue was purchased by the United States Department of Agriculture and it became the USDA Experimental Center, or "beetle lab," where scientists worked on methods to stop the invasive Japanese beetle.

C.A. Lippincott & Bro. was located at the corner of Third and Union Streets next to the railroad. The view in this c. 1910 photograph is looking toward Church Street from Union Street. The company sold paint, glass, and other building supplies, as well as coal, animal feed, and flour. The company remains in business today as Lippincott Supply Company but is no longer located in Moorestown.

In 1868, Jones Yerkes opened a canning factory at the north end of Schooley Street, where he produced 30,000 gallons of tomato ketchup annually. In 1878, the H.K. & F.B. Thurber & Company bought Yerkes's factory and produced its Baldwin brand of ketchup there. Advertising campaigns of the time marketed to high-end clientele, trying to overcome the general population's skepticism of the food they could not see or smell. The ketchup was sold in decanter-style bottles at $2.50 a quart. (Courtesy of MIA.)

Measey's Hardware, shown above around 1890, was located at 132 West Main Street at the corner of Church Street. Frederick Measey was also a tin-roofing contractor. As far back as 1825, there was a store located on this site. The building was demolished to make way for a gas station in the mid-1900s. W.H. Slocum Marble and Granite works, shown below around 1890, was at 65–67 East Main Street. It supplied headstones and grave markers for area residents. Its rear workshop, shown at the far left, was at 65 East Main Street and no longer exists; the home built in 1850 at 67 East Main Street, however, is used as office space today.

Built on the southwest corner of Mill and Second Streets in 1849, Buzby's Mill burned down in 1857 and was rebuilt. John C. Hopkins bought the gristmill in 1867. On maps from 1900, the location is called Moorestown Roller Mills, as mechanization had been introduced. The photograph above shows some of the Hopkins Mill employees outside the building. By 1925, the structure was home to Ellis Plumbing. The photograph below shows Ellis's employees and the company trucks in 1926.

Located on the corner of Chester Avenue and Third Street, Frank Laessle's Groceries was a purveyor of fine foods, as can be seen in the c. 1900 photograph below of the interior of the store. Shopping was done by the lady of the house, who selected the family's preferred foods with basket in hand. She would give a time to the clerk as to when she would be home, and the grocer would box up the requested items, load them in the horse-drawn carriage, and deliver them to her door. The building, located at 301 Chester Avenue, was built in 1890 and is owned today by the Moorestown Friends School. (Above, courtesy of MIA; below, courtesy of Moorestown Community House.)

The building located at 131 West Main Street on the corner of Church Street has a rather interesting past. Since about 1875, it has been a grocery store, first owned by George Heaton. It was then the home of W.I. Newbold & Son Cash Grocer, shown above around 1910. By 1920, it was the home of Wolff's Market, whose delivery truck is shown below. It is currently the home of Ralph's Market. In January 1881, the Chester Club formed for recreational purposes and met on the second floor of Heaton's store. This was a gentlemen's private club and it had very strict rules disallowing alcohol or gambling of any sort. The club was richly furnished and appointed, and no mention can be found of its demise. (Both, courtesy of MIA.)

Deacon's Meat Market, built and owned by Abraham Deacon, was in operation before 1886. The market, shown in the c. 1900 photograph above, was located at what is now 35 East Main Street on property that went through to Second Street. By the 1940s, the property was owned by A.J. Deacon, who ran not only the meat market, but also the Moorestown roller rink, which sat behind the market with an entrance on Second Street. It could also be reached via an alley that ran alongside the market, which is today known as Deacon's Alley. When the rink was demolished in the mid-1960s, the salvaged lumber was used to build twin houses on East Second Street near Mill Street. Locust Lane Dairy, whose c. 1925 advertisement is pictured at left, was located at Third and Mill Streets just north of the railroad. It is now the home of Tait Roofing. (Both, courtesy of MIA.)

The MacAllister Machine Shop, shown above around 1910, was located at 228 Chester Avenue, where the Laessle Building is today. The sign reads "Automobile and Bicycle Manufacturer and Repairer." Later, a gasoline tank was installed for a pump at the curb. The building on the left was demolished to build the firehouse extension in 1974. The c. 1936 scene below shows East Main Street in a view looking east toward the Burlington County Trust Company Building, where the clock is visible at front. The three-story buildings were demolished in the 1960s for the bank's drive-thru expansion. The Moorestown Five and Dime is on the left, with Stiles Pharmacy next door. (Both, courtesy of MIA.)

East Main Street, Moorestown, N. J.

Thomas Dolly & Sons Chevrolet dealership and Texaco station, pictured above in 1924, was located at the corner of East Main Street and Borton Landing Road. In October 1924, Chevrolet sponsored a 100-hour endurance economy run for Chevrolet dealers across the country to showcase the attributes of the new Chevrolet touring car. The Thomas Dolly & Sons entry is shown below. The entrants used four drivers to be sure that the car was never idle, as mileage and gas consumption were checked before and after the run. There were guessing contests, and cash prizes were offered to the winners.

Moorestown Motor Company, pictured above in the 1940s, was located at 219 West Main Street. Constructed around 1875, the building was a car dealership for decades, and was modernized often. In June 1952, the house that was located at 217 West Main Street, known as the Ferg House, was prepared to roll down the street to its new home on Kings Highway to make way for the expansion of Duncan Buick, which occupied the spot until 1981. In 1999, the property was sold to CVS Pharmacy, which demolished the old building.

The residence located at 1 West Main Street was built in 1858 by John Buzby. John's brother William Buzby owned the old mill located behind the house at Mill and Second Streets that burned down in 1857. John purchased the property from his brother and built a new gristmill on the site. He sold the mill to John C. Hopkins in 1867. The Buzby House has been many things over the years. At various times, it was an inn, a yarn shop, the Vanity Beauty Salon in the 1920s, an insurance agency, and, in 1941, the Rulon Hotel.

The Coles Hotel, built in 1800, once stood at 91 East Main Street next to the Friends cemetery. It was demolished in 1926 to make way for the new Burlington County Trust Company bank building, shown here. Simon and Simon Architects of Philadelphia designed the bank building.

On the northwest corner of West Main Street and North Washington Avenue stood Tippenhauer's Butcher shop, likely built around 1850. The butcher shop is named on the 1896 map along with a tin shop in the rear. Wilkinson's West End Pharmacy, shown here in 1900, took over the building. The pharmacy placed an advertisement in the March 1905 edition of the Moorestown Improvement Association paper with the suggestion to take "beef, wine, and iron for a good spring tonic."

The Criterion Theater, located at 5 West Main Street, was opened by J.B. Fox in 1920, when a Marr and Colton organ was installed. The theater was closed in the mid-1950s and reopened as the Carlton Theater in 1959, although it closed again in 1963. The building was sold and reopened for a short time as the Moorestown Playhouse, a live theater venue. (Courtesy of Allen Hauss.)

Witcraft's Restaurant was located at 103 West Main Street. The window sign notes that it has "Tables for Ladies" and "Oysters in Every Style." Oysters must have been a new delicacy for Virginia Root of California, who was visiting the DeCou family in 1904. She mentions repeatedly in her letters the wonderful oyster dishes served at all the best house parties.

H.B. Gale Steam Laundry was located at 315 North Washington Avenue, behind what is now Moorestown Hardware at the end of the train track siding. In the photograph, a laundry worker loads the large washers. The laundry is listed on the 1905 map and was in operation until at least 1955.

The Burlington County Aero Club (Municipal) Field was dedicated in 1928 on a 50-acre field purchased from the Lippincott farm on Westfield Road. Run by the Burlington County Aero Club, the field had a steel hangar, two Waco biplanes, and a full-time chief pilot and instructor. The complex eventually grew into a three-runway airport (shown here around 1950) complete with two hangars, outbuildings, and a luncheonette. The airport officially closed on November 1, 1973, due to residential encroachment that prohibited its growth. At the time of its closing, it was the second-oldest airport in New Jersey. (Courtesy of MIA.)

EW JERSEY, WEDNESDAY, DEC

MOORESTOWN IS STILL IN RUNNING AS AIR BASE SITE

International Zeppelin Transport Officials Deny Statement of Eckener

FIELD NOT ELIMINATED IN "ZEP" CONSIDERATION

No Decision Until Congress Gives Dirigibles Status as Mail Carriers

Officials of the International Zeppelin Corporation Monday denied that Moorestown has been eliminated from consideration as a probable American terminal for the proposed trans-Atlantic airship line, as indicated by Dr. Hugo Eckener.

In this article from December 30, 1931, one can see that Moorestown Airport was in the final running to be a base for a transatlantic zeppelin mail route. Trips would have taken three days from Moorestown to Europe. Lakehurst Naval Air Station won the contract for the zeppelin mail route, which began in 1936 but was disbanded entirely after the Hindenburg disaster on May 6, 1937. (Courtesy of MIA.)

75

Several private bus companies were run in Moorestown. One bus company was located at 123 East Second Street and ran round-trip from Moorestown to Riverton. The bus pictured in the c. 1940 image above ran from Philadelphia to Moorestown. Radio Corporation of America (RCA)—which included the Victor Talking Machine Company, founded by Eldridge R. Johnson—came to Moorestown in 1953 and opened its plant on 430 acres on the rural east end of town. Although it has changed its name over the years (it is now Lockheed Martin), the plant has long been a big presence in town. In 1959, RCA developed and installed a radar station inside a gigantic "golf ball," or radome. The 15-story-tall, 140-foot-wide snow-white ball was the first one built in the United States and a familiar landmark to all those who grew up in the area. In 1974, the ball was replaced with the "Cruiser in the Cornfield," also know as the "USS Rancocas" and the US Navy's Aegis Combat System testing facility, officially the Vice Admiral James H. Doyle Combat Systems Engineering Development Site. (Both, courtesy of MIA.)

Seven

FIRE DEPARTMENTS

Following the Great Fire of London in 1666, insurance companies sprang up offering to insure property against fire for a small monthly fee. A painted cast-iron marker was hung on the home to display that the house was insured. Brought to the colonies by English settlers, the practice proliferated here. This is an ad for the G.C. Gillespie Company from the May 1905 Moorestown Improvement Association newsletter. A fire association emblem can still be seen on the house at 400 East Main Street. (Courtesy of MIA.)

Incorporated in 1888, the first home of Hose Company No. 1 was on West Second Street on school property. In 1893, it moved to its new building on North Washington Avenue, shown above with its state-of-the-art ladder truck. From there, the fire company moved in 1916 to 215 West Main Street and then to its current location at 261 West Main Street. Hose Company No. 2 was incorporated in 1890. Its first home was an old building at East Main Street and Zelley Avenue. In 1891, it moved to Third Street and Elm Avenue, where it rechartered as Relief Engine Company, shown below. Its final move was to 222 Chester Avenue, where it remains.

The structure in the above c. 1900 photograph sat behind the Coles Hotel on East Main Street among the buildings of Dugan's Wagon Works. It housed the hand-operated water pumper for Hose Company No. 1. The Franklin No. 1760 is shown below around 1900. This is the original pump that was stored on the Dugan's Wagon Works property.

Relief Engine Company, pictured here in September 1923, shows off its new 1922 Ahrens Fox fire truck that was equipped as both a pumper and ladder truck, complete with bell and spotlight. The truck, known as "Bertha," is still housed at the Chester Avenue fire station. Pictured standing on the left are Bun and Al Ellis. Chief Ellis MacAllister is in the center in the light coat.

The canteen truck belonging to Relief Engine Company is shown at the Riverside High School fire around 1950. The canteen was used to carry drinking water, blankets, extra equipment, and personnel.

The Lenola Fire Company, shown here behind the company's first two fire trucks, was chartered in 1922 and had its first home at 9 North Lenola Road. The company's first fire truck, a Ford Model T chemical truck (on the right), was purchased in 1923 and retired in 1934. The truck at left is an early converted hearse of similar vintage that was used as an ambulance. (Courtesy of Moorestown Fire District No. 2.)

The Lenola Fire Company, shown here in 1938, provides fire protection for Fire District No. 2, the west end of Moorestown, which now includes the Moorestown Industrial Park, the Moorestown Mall, and many other commercial properties. It also provides mutual aid for the other town fire departments. (Courtesy of Moorestown Fire District No. 2.)

Lenola Fire Company took part in the celebration marking 200 years of continuous service by volunteer firemen held in Mount Holly, New Jersey, in 1952. (Courtesy of MIA.)

The Lenola Fire Company moved to its current home at 229 North Lenola Road in 1961. The Lenola Fire Company ladder truck is shown inside the Moorestown Mall during an exhibition in 1970. The company received the 1970 award for Best Appearing Aerial Ladder from the New Jersey State Fire Convention. (Courtesy of Moorestown Fire District No. 2.)

Eight

COMMUNITY SERVICES

Following the typhoid epidemic of 1912, the Moorestown Improvement Association was instrumental in the digging of artesian wells and the building of new water towers to improve the quality of the drinking water. This c. 1913 photograph shows the new steel water tower being pulled along Main Street to its permanent location on the south side of East Main Street across from Zelley Avenue, where the wooden water tower stood.

The Friends began a subscription library with one book placed in John Buzby's Main Street shop. Patrons could borrow books when the shop was open. Not until 1879 did the library find a permanent home, at the Friends Academy, where the children's book collection was started. A class picture shows the students in 1880 in front of the library. (Courtesy of Moorestown Friends School.)

The library was moved to its home at the newly completed Moorestown Community House in 1926 and remained there until 1971, when it moved to its new building at Church and Second Streets. (Courtesy of Moorestown Community House.)

The Moorestown Field Club, shown in this c. 1895 photograph, was founded in 1892 to encourage "ball playing, cricket playing, and other moral, healthful physical exercise." In 1898, it built a nine-hole golf course in an apple orchard on the west side of Chester Avenue. In 1910, member Samuel Allen developed plans for a more interesting nine-hole course on the east side of Chester Avenue behind the tennis courts.

The 1902 Moorestown Field Club cricket team is shown above. One of the events of the year at the club was the "ladies" team day, where the male club members played baseball at the club while dressed as ladies. The real ladies came to watch, cheer, and picnic in the shade. The club building was moved and altered in 1923, and the current field house was rebuilt again in 1969.

The Order of the Patrons of Husbandry was founded in 1867 to advance the social and economic status of farmers and their families. It was founded by Oliver H. Kelly, an official of the Department of Agriculture in Washington, DC. Bimonthly meetings were held by local chapters, known as Granges. Shown in this c. 1880 image, the Moorestown Grange picnic was a social event for the farming families of the area. The Grange Hall, built in 1886, still stands at 123 East Main Street.

It was the lamplighter's job to light streetlamps at dusk each evening. Early gaslights, invented in England in the 1790s, became popular in the United States in the early part of the 1800s. During the early days, it was necessary to light the gas lamps by hand. In later years, a system was developed to automatically turn on the lamps. Here, a lamplighter is at work in Moorestown around 1885.

As noted in the minutes of its meeting of October 15, 1909, the Moorestown Improvement Association voted to purchase from "John Manion his lot at the junction of Camden Pike and Second Street for a public park" for $500. The lot, shown in this c. 1900 photograph, was landscaped and maintained by the organization until 1918. At that time, it was dedicated as Remembrance Park in memory of the seven patriotic men from town who died in World War I. It was given to the township at that time. In 1994, American Legion Post No. 42 rededicated the park.

Katherine Condon was a Red Cross volunteer at Camp Dix during World War I. She is pictured in her uniform at her home at 308 West Main Street around 1918.

The first meeting of Rotary International's Moorestown chapter was held on April 2, 1925, at the Coles Hotel, and 25 days later, on May 6, 1925, the charter meeting was held and the bylaws passed. The 23 charter members are shown here, including John G. Pettit, treasurer of the Moorestown Trust Company and club president. (Courtesy of Moorestown Community House.)

This c. 1955 photograph shows Percy Lovell, publisher of the *Moorestown News Chronicle*, with two unidentified ladies who are about to deliver a welcome package to new residents of the village. Local businesses donated coupons and advertisements for the new residents. A copy of the newspaper can be seen in the basket.

Mail delivery in Moorestown began in 1893. Prior to that time, residents had to stop at the post office to pick up their mail. Shown here in 1908 is an early Moorestown mail delivery truck, with postmaster Evan Benners on the right and Benjamin Heal, assistant postmaster, on the left.

Pictured is postmaster George Gibson, who held the position from 1933 to 1951. In 1938, he swore in Robert N. Hunt, a Moorestown pilot, as he prepared to carry the first airmail letters sent from Moorestown's airport. Special airmail cachets featuring historical Moorestown were carried on that first flight. Paul Evans drove the mail to the airport in an official mail truck. (Courtesy of OLGC.)

Mrs. Alfred W. Sumner founded the Moorestown Visiting Nurse Association in 1904 with the support of the Moorestown Women's Club. The board president, Mrs. Nathan Thorne, represented the organization on the committee to built the Moorestown Community House in 1926, where the association found a permanent home. Shown here in 1938 is a visiting nurse on her rounds.

The Moorestown Improvement Association played a pivotal role in procuring WPA money and contracts to dam the north branch of the Pennsauken Creek to create the Strawbridge Lake Park, pictured in 1939. In 1931, during the Depression, the Moorestown Improvement Association raised funds to hire 15 unemployed townsmen to trim trees, paint street signs, and to do general cleanup and gardening work in the town. (Courtesy of MIA.)

The Moorestown Improvement Association's decorated truck is shown here in 1913 promoting the group's annual Clean Up Day. The truck was owned by Martin Dugan of Moorestown. On one such Clean Up Day in 1926, volunteers removed 90 loads of trash. (Courtesy of MIA.)

The Moorestown Community House, built in 1926, was the center of activities in the town. The old gym was the site of many meetings and dinners, including this one, a c. 1940 banquet for Trinity Episcopal Church. (Courtesy of Moorestown Community House.)

The West End Community Center, which was located on North Church Street (now Yancy-Adams Park), was the center of activity for the adjacent neighborhoods for many years. This bride and groom are shown leaving their reception in 1956. (Courtesy of MIA.)

The Kings Highway Water Treatment Plant for the artesian well was built in 1914. This c. 1940 photograph was taken after the redbrick building was painted white. There was also an outdoor community pool at this location that was open for children during the summer months, as swimming in the lake was discouraged. (Courtesy of MIA.)

The police station, the small white building shown at the right in 1970, was the second home of the force. It was on the property of Dugan's Wagon Works and may have previously been used by Dugan as a woodshop. The first police station was in Old Town Hall, located at 40 East Main Street, where the records show that an addition for the jail was made in 1876. The police eventually relocated into the larger building, shown at left, before moving to the new municipal building at Church and Second Streets. (Courtesy of MIA.)

The building on the north side of Second Street, shown in this c. 1970 image, was the home of township offices until it was demolished to make way for the municipal complex in 1971.

Sledding on Stokes Hill has been a township tradition and rite of passage for generations. Samuel Leeds Allen, inventor of the Flexible Flyer sled, tried his initial attempts at a new type of sled near his home in Westtown, now Cinnaminson, but he needed a longer hill. In looking for such a hill, he discovered the slope on East Main Street in Moorestown across the street from the land he owned. His daughter, Elizabeth Roberts Allen, relates in the 1920 biography *Samuel L. Allen: Intimate Recollections & Letters*: "By removing a panel of fence we could get nearly a quarter-mile run." The hill was named for a Stokes family that lived adjacent to the hill, and generations of sledders assumed that the township owned the property. The township finally bought the land in January 1993 from the owner, who had purchased it as an investment. The Moorestown Improvement Association helped the township raise funds for the purchase. This c. 1970 photograph shows sledding on Stokes Hill. (Courtesy of MIA.)

Nine

HOMES AND
STREET SCENES

The original brick portion of the house located at 406 Kings Highway, shown in this c. 1890 image, was built in 1740. Later frame additions were done in the late 1700s for owners John and Sarah Lippincott. In the mid-1800s, the property was purchased by John Perkins, co-owner of Fairview Nurseries, now the Perkins Arboretum. In 1894, it was acquired by Edward Strawbridge of the Strawbridge and Clothier fortune, who named the estate Pinehurst. He raised cattle on the south portion of the property, which extended to what is now Strawbridge Lake.

Thomas Moore, for whom Moorestown is named, came to Chester Township in 1734 and opened his tavern and hotel at what is now 274 West Main Street. In 1878, Joseph Lippincott razed the tavern and built the house shown in the c. 1900 image above. The home was later demolished to make way for a gas station. The house at the southeast corner of Church and Second Streets, in the c. 1920 photograph below, was built sometime after 1880 at the site of Moorestown's first public school. On the far left in the photograph are the stately Victorian-era homes that were demolished to make room for the municipal parking lot on Second Street in 1956. Note the wooden curbs, tiny US postbox, and the hitching post in the photograph.

Thomas Ewing built the original house at 16 East Main Street in 1804. In 1838, it was purchased by Dr. Samuel Thornton, who enlarged the house, created verandas, and planted a large garden and orchard. It was considered one of the most notable mansions of Moorestown. Mary Sumner was the final resident of the house, shown above around 1910, before it was demolished to make way for the Moorestown Community House in 1926. The house shown below around 1920 was built in 1904 and located at 105 East Main Street. It was demolished to make way for the Bell Telephone Building in 1955. This location was the original site of Cox's Tavern, which was built in 1745.

The oldest portion of the Zelley farmhouse off of North Stanwick Road, shown above in 1929, was built in 1721. The farm was originally part of a tract of land William Penn granted in 1677 to William Biddle, who sold it to Dr. Thomas Rodman in 1686. It passed into the Zelley family in 1782. The 237-acre Zelley farm was eventually developed as Oak and Central Avenues, including Pearl and Elm Streets. The area south of the Kings Highway was farmland well into the 20th century. Below is a photograph of Dr. Thorne's cow standing in the field below the Ridge in 1897. The view is looking up Pages Lane toward the Friends Meeting House. (Courtesy of Moorestown Friends School.)

Built in 1855 by Jonathan Williams, the estate located at 730 Riverton Road was sold in the early 1900s to Mr. and Mrs. William R. Rhoads, who named it Hereshome Farm. This estate of over 100 acres was never a working farm, but rather a country estate. Even today, the original long entrance road is marked by a double row of pear trees. During winter snowstorms, the best, and most fun, way of transportation was the horse-drawn sleigh. Below, a family sleighs on Riverton Road around 1890.

The Kings Highway was originally laid out in 1682. Its path was altered slightly over the years to accommodate village growth. In 1796, the road west of Pleasant Valley Avenue was diverted to the south. On the left is a c. 1880 view of the original right-of-way on the Matlack farm. The house that was located on the northeast corner of West Main and Locust Streets, shown in the c. 1900 image below, was on the original Thomas French tract. The style of the structure puts the construction date in the late 1700s or early 1800s. The house was demolished in 1940 to make way for the Pine Tree Apartments.

Harmony Hall, the home at 607 Chester Avenue shown in the c. 1890 image above, was built in 1753 by the Honorable Samuel Stokes, a colonial assemblyman. It became the home of several generations of Stokes physicians, ending with Dr. John Hinchman Stokes II in 1873. Dr. Stokes was such a strong believer in Edward Jenner's theory of vaccination that he inoculated his little daughter Hannah with the cowpox vaccine and laid her in a bed with a smallpox sufferer to prove to the town that the injection would work. She did not contract the disease. He was the first physician in Burlington County to use the vaccine. The c. 1910 photograph below shows friends motoring on Kings Highway west of Pleasant Valley Avenue.

The Dr. Samuel Haines house located at 124 East Main Street was built in 1756, with a rear addition constructed in 1860. Shown in the c. 1930 image above, it was the site of the very first meeting, held in 1808, for the formation of the Moorestown Library Company, which sought to "promote useful knowledge and Christian values." Pictured below, the Alfred H. Burr House was built at 37 East Main Street in 1860. The house, which had been on the property for more than 100 years, was moved by John Manion to West Second Street. Burr was a storeowner, the postmaster (for a short time), and one of the original builders of twin homes on Second Street.

E.C. Worrell had a plumbing business and tin shop at 309 Chester Avenue from the late 1800s into the 1900s. The house was built in 1882 and is shown here in 1926 with its original wraparound porch. Most of the residences on and around Chester Avenue were built from 1880 to 1890, a time of opulent construction of grand Victorian homes. Central Avenue is approximately the location of the original dirt lane that led to the farmhouse owned by Amos Stiles. His 100 acres were parceled into large lots and sold to a group headed by J.S. Collins for development. The c. 1900 view below is on Chester Avenue at Central Avenue looking toward the railroad. The bell tower of the original Presbyterian church can be seen in the center. (Both, courtesy of MIA.)

Sweeping lawns and wide porches were the order of the day and are still evident in the homes that remain on Chester Avenue and the surrounding blocks. In this c. 1900 image, a couple is seen starting out for a stroll on the wide drive that leads to a carriage house in the rear of the property at 328 Chester Avenue.

Dr. J. Boon Wintersteen shows off his new touring car in front of his home at 417 Chester Avenue. The east side of Chester Avenue, north of the railroad from Third Street to Oak Avenue and east to Elm Street, was developed by a group of 10 businessmen following the building of the railroad in 1867. The area was known as "the Company Grounds." (Courtesy of MIA.)

The Kennard home was on the southwest corner of Central Avenue and Chestnut Street. Here, a group of children poses for a photograph in 1895. A Halloween party given in 1904 is recounted in a letter written by a houseguest of the DeCou family, Virginia Root, who was visiting from California, where she relates the menu, games, and fun that was had. The letters are in the collection of the Historical Society of Moorestown. (Courtesy of Moorestown Friends School.)

The area on Chester Avenue north of Oak Avenue was developed after the turn of the 20th century. This 1910 photograph of the N. Newlin Stokes home, located at 601 Chester Avenue, shows a Shingle Style home, with more sweeping eaves, lower rooflines, and less ornamentation than other Victorian styles, but still with large covered porches and grand elegance.

Breidenhart Castle, whose name means "broad hearthstone" or "hospitality," was built by Samuel Leeds Allen in 1894. It was designed by noted Philadelphia architect Walter Smedley, a fellow Quaker who had been an apprentice under Addison Hutton, designer of the additions to the Strawbridge Mansion on Kings Highway. Built in the Romanesque Revival style, its ornamentation can be seen in the various textures and colors of the stone. Allen, who was granted nearly 300 patents for farm implements, is best known for having invented the Flexible Flyer sled in 1889. He lived in the house until his death in 1918. Eldridge Reeves Johnson, founder of the Victor Talking Machine Company, purchased the house in 1920 and lived there until his death in 1945. Although Johnson made no exterior changes to the home, he did install finely detailed interior wood trims. Following Johnson's death, his widow sold the home and 12-acre property to the Lutheran Home of New Jersey, which has added several wings and buildings. The building is listed in the National Register of Historic Places. (Courtesy of MIA.)

In 1734, Nehemiah Haines purchased 179 acres of land in the village of Moorestown. His grandson John C. Haines built the original one-room home located at 245 East Main Street in 1800; it is now known as the Haines-Spencer house (above center). In 1818, Dr. Jonathan Spencer, brother-in-law of Edward Harris, purchased the property and greatly enlarged the home. On the left in the c. 1900 photograph above is the Gillingham house, built in 1874 of randomly coursed brownstone in the Gothic Revival style. On the far right is Breidenhart Castle, although the stone blends so well into the landscape that it is hard to see. Built by Ephraim Haines in 1760, with additions done by Samuel Haines in 1825, the house shown below in 1926 sits today at 201 East Main Street.

In 1815, at the fork of the road where Camden Avenue meets Kings Highway, John French and John Perkins established Fairview Nurseries, specializing in ornamental trees. Following the wedding of Perkins's grandson T.H. Dudley Perkins to Alice Sullivan, the house now known as Perkins Center for the Arts was built as a gift by Dudley's parents in 1910. Designed by architect Herbert C. Wise, the Tudor Revival home was inspired by English country manor houses and was named Evergreen Lawn. When Dudley died in the influenza epidemic in 1918, Alice and their son T. H. Dudley Jr. invited her sister Mabel and her husband to live with them. Mabel purchased the home from the younger Dudley's estate after his tragic death at age 48. Upon her death, Mabel bequeathed the property to the township "to be used in perpetuity as a park." The property was to always remain as open space for the community. In the early 1970s, the property was listed in the National Register of Historic Places and was to be used as a self-sustaining cultural arts center.

In the early village, the area north of Main Street was a thick oak forest. In 1840, the forest was cut back and Second Street, a residential thoroughfare, was laid out. The houses were set close to the street, all with front porches and many with fruit trees, shrubs, and flower gardens. The house at 51 East Second Street (above) was built around 1850 in the classic colonial style. It still retains its original metal roof today. The house at 41 East Second Street (below), also built in 1851, is a Greek Revival town house. The street was dotted with similar homes, on smaller lots compared to the grander mansions on Chester Avenue. Both photographs date to about 1880.

The section of town along Stanwick Road, originally part of the Zelley farm, was built in the 1880s and 1890s. The Queen Anne style is evident here. The residence at 405 East Second Street, at far left in the above c. 1900 photograph, was built in 1890 for the president of the Camden & Amboy Railroad. The lush wood trims and floors throughout the interior of the home are evidence of its first owner's wealth and station. The house at 202 West Main Street, shown in the c. 1900 image below, was built by Samuel C. Thornton Jr. in 1886. The property was part of the original John Rodman tract of 533 acres in West Moorestown that was deeded in 1686.

J.S. Collins once owned the house located at the point of Chester Avenue and Bridgeboro Road. After his death, the family left it to the Presbyterian church, which built its sanctuary in front of it and its Sunday school building behind. The original building is now almost unrecognizable. Even in the 1800s, snow removal was a laborious task. In the c. 1895 photograph below, a gentleman uses a team of horses to plow the snow on town sidewalks.

In 1888, J.S. Rogers laid out a street to run between Mill Street and Lippincott Avenue, originally to be called Fourth Street. When he submitted plans for the row houses to be built, the name of the road had been changed to Beech Street. In order to house the Irish immigrants who worked at the mill owned by J.S. Collins, 20 connected houses were built on the site in 1892. The block was destroyed in a major fire in the 1970s and was later rebuilt. (Courtesy of MIA.)

The Great Blizzard of 1888, which occurred from March 11 to March 14, was the worst East Coast blizzard in US history. The storm dropped nearly 40 inches of snow, downing telegraph wires and blocking railways. This photograph shows local men gathered to clear the train tracks at Wilson Station, near Lenola Road.

Children ride on Dr. Nathan Thorne's wagon on Chester Avenue near the Moorestown Friends High School around 1880. Having to cross the muddy streets meant a messy commute to school. (Courtesy of Moorestown Friends School.)

The Great Hurricane of 1938 was possibly the largest and most deadly ever to hit the East Coast. Although most of the destruction done by the Category 3 storm was in New York and New England, it caused damage and major flooding throughout New Jersey. Overall, the hurricane was estimated to have killed between 680 and 800 people and damaged or destroyed over 57,000 homes. This photograph shows flooding caused by the storm on Winthrop Avenue in the Lenola section of town. Note that there is a person on the pole in the upper right. (Courtesy of MIA.)

Main Street in Moorestown was a bustling village center in the late 1800s, with carriages and trolley cars going up and down the dusty dirt streets. The view in the c. 1890 photograph above is looking toward Chester Avenue, with the Alfred Burr house in the left foreground. The house second from left was Mortland Meat Market, which was demolished to make way for the Moorestown Trust Company building, now a Starbucks. The c. 1890 photograph below shows one of the town's country lanes, with bicyclists on both the dirt road and the dirt sidewalk. (Both, courtesy of MIA.)

Ten

PEOPLE AND NOTABLES

Dr. Mary E. Roberts taught English at the Moorestown High School from 1912 to 1919. In 1920, she was selected to be the high school principal, a position she held for 33 years. The programs she implemented and the excellence she demanded took the high school to the highest ranking in the state. Dr. Roberts was the first recipient of the Rose Foundation Excellence in Education Award for South Jersey in 1948. She was loved and respected by her students and her staff. Upon her retirement in 1953, the alumni association presented her with a new car. An elementary school was named in her honor in 1957.

Alice Sullivan Perkins (left), her son T.H. Dudley Jr., her sister Mabel, and Francis D'Olier (at the crank) are ready to set off on a motoring adventure from the carriage house behind their home at 395 Kings Highway in 1932. The family raised Saint Bernards, cocker spaniels, and homing pigeons, and had a large kitchen garden, which is now a community garden space. The tiny house near the garden was built as the pigeon house. (Courtesy of Perkins Center for the Arts.)

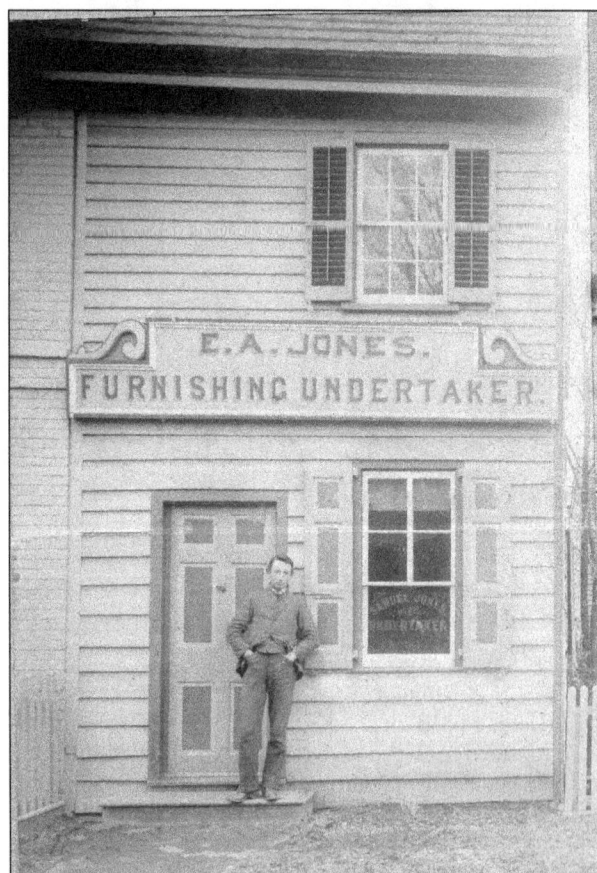

Trained by his father, William, in the family shop on East Main Street, Samuel Jones was a carpenter. He moved his shop to 78 East Main Street, where he devoted his time to undertaking for the next 50 years. He was among the first wardens of Trinity Episcopal Church and a prominent Moorestown businessman. (Courtesy of Moorestown Community House.)

Percy Lovell became the owner and editor of the *Moorestown Chronicle* in 1934. The weekly newspaper's office was on the west side of Chester Avenue, at the present location of Relief Engine Company. Lovell is shown above in the newspaper office around 1950. An integral and well-respected member of the community for many years, he died in 1957.

David Bispham was born in Philadelphia in 1857 and moved with his family to Moorestown when he was 10 years old. He graduated from the Friends School, where he performed in musicals, and from Haverford College in 1876. He had no formal musical training but performed in the Episcopal choir in Philadelphia. At age 28, he studied in Europe and became the first American opera singer to win international acclaim. Bispham died in 1921. (Courtesy of Library of Congress.)

George DeCou was born in 1867 to Samuel and Sarah DeCou on their dairy farm near Trenton, New Jersey. He came to Chester Township as a student at the Westtown Boarding School. After his schooling, he learned the shoe business working in his brother's Trenton firm and at age 20 became its traveling salesman. George and his brother opened their own wholesale shoe business on Market Street in Philadelphia in 1890. George married Margaret Daniels in 1891. They owned several homes in Moorestown, including 114 East Oak Avenue, where they raised their six daughters. His shoe enterprise was liquidated in 1931, and George retired from business. He loved local history and soon became the president and historian for the Burlington County Historical Society. He was an organizer and first president of the Moorestown Improvement Association, founded in 1904.

Although Moorestown has its roots in the Quaker traditions, it did not escape the brutality of war. Moorestown's surviving Civil War veterans are shown on the steps of Old Town Hall in this c. 1900 photograph. (Courtesy of Moorestown Community House.)

Moorestown son William H. Snyder joined the US Army and sailed for England in June 1918. Private Snyder was killed on October 3, 1918, in the Meuse-Argonne Offensive. The Moorestown chapter of the American Legion was named in his honor.

Scouting was founded in England in 1908, and within two years, the Boy Scouts of America was incorporated and its first National Council selected. Within just a few years, various youth organizations across the country had been melded into the program. Early Scouting was not without controversy, but the program endured and grew. Moorestown Boy Scout Troop No. 2 is shown here in 1919.

A men's hunting group is shown at Paulsdale on Hooten Road following a rabbit hunt in 1950. Percy Lovell is standing second from right.

Located at 69 East Main Street, Thomas Cannavo's barbershop was the ultimate in customer service. The rear wall of the shop, shown above in 1923, was lined with customer's personal shaving mugs and brushes. (Courtesy of Moorestown Community House.)

The Zelley family, like many at Christmas, gathered at the old homestead to celebrate the season. Even the family dog is included. Chalkey and Mary Zelley are seated in this 1913 photograph.

May Day has been celebrated as the beginning of spring since ancient times. Most of the modern rituals come from the Gaelic Beltane celebration, with dancing around the maypole and crowning of the May Queen. The day took on new meaning with the unionization of workers in the United States and the acceptance of a five-day workweek. May Day celebrations were common in the 19th century, and they were held at the Moorestown Field Club and at the Moorestown Friends Academy. Shown are c. 1921 (above) and c. 1930 (below) photographs of May Day celebrations at the Friends Academy. (Both, courtesy of Moorestown Friends School)

Catherine Kerlin's family moved to Moorestown in 1917 when she was 11 years old. She attended Moorestown Friends School and Smith College and traveled in Europe working for the diplomatic corps. Along the way, she met Amos Wilder. On June 26, 1935, the couple was married in the garden of her parents' home at 200 East Central Avenue. Amos's younger brother Thornton, who served as best man, can be seen standing at far right in this photograph. It is stated in Thornton Wilder's biography that he began writing the wedding scene for the play *Our Town* on July 2, shortly after his brother's wedding. A collection of memorabilia from the wedding can be seen at the Historical Society of Moorestown.

Lydia Babbott was born and raised in New York, graduated from Vassar in 1917, and worked with the Girl Reserves at the YMCA in Brooklyn. In 1920, she married S. Emlen Stokes, a Moorestown pediatrician, and move to the mansion at Chester Avenue and Bridgeboro Road. She was deeply committed to philanthropic causes and served on the boards of the Moorestown Visiting Nurse Association and the American Friends Service Committee for 15 years. She donated funds for the building of Stokes Hall at the Moorestown Friends School and the Stokes Pavilion at Memorial Hospital of Burlington County. She died in 1988 at the age of 93. (Courtesy of Bachrach Photography, Philadelphia, PA.)

Quilting bees, as shown in this c. 1880 image, were quite common. Piecing a quilt top with leftover or salvaged fabrics was artistic and fun, but the actual quilting could be laborious. Gathering with family and friends made the work lighter.

Beloved Moorestown physician Dr. Joseph Stokes is shown near the bicycle he pedaled all over town to make his house calls on sick patients. The c. 1890 scene shows a view looking west on West Main Street toward the fork at Camden Avenue. Stokes's home at 607 Chester Avenue was built in 1753 by his great-great-grandfather.

Eldridge Reeves Johnson did not move to Moorestown until 1920, years after founding the Victor Talking Machine Company (later RCA), but his impact on the community cannot be denied. He donated funds to build the Moorestown Community House, still the center of town activity; for the expansion of the Trinity Episcopal Church; and the house that was to become the Evergreens Retirement Home. (Courtesy of Moorestown Community House.)

In 1885, Alice Paul was born at Paulsdale, her family homestead, in Evesham Township, now Mount Laurel. The eldest child of Hicksite Quaker parents, Alice was raised to believe in gender equality and the need to work toward a better society. She was both an outstanding student and athlete at the Moorestown Friends High School (shown below) and graduated first in her class in 1901. After graduating from Swarthmore College in 1905, she joined the suffragist movement while studying in England. Back in the United States, she joined the Women's Suffrage Association and was imprisoned for her activities. On August 6, 1920, the Nineteenth Amendment granting women the right to vote was ratified. In 1923, Paul authored the Equal Rights Amendment and worked for its passage until her death in 1977. (Left, courtesy of Library of Congress; below, courtesy of Moorestown Friends School.)

About MIA

Moorestown Improvement Association (MIA) began with a meeting of 40 citizens representing all sections of town at the home of William E. Rhoads on Oak Avenue. All in attendance at the meeting were in agreement that an organization whose aim was to "enhance the quality of life in Moorestown" would benefit the town. The MIA was formed in 1904 and became officially incorporated in 1909. It is the oldest civic organization in Moorestown and remains dedicated to preserving and enhancing the community. Below is a sampling of the organization's 110-year history.

1904	Published free, monthly newspaper called *Village Improvement*
1905	Replaced boardwalks with first concrete and brick sidewalks
1907	Planted first shade trees (this program continues annually to the present day)
1909	Installed street signs (until 1922); first athletic field on South Church Street
1910	Purchased and landscaped what would become Remembrance Park
1912	Initiated first artesian wells and erected first water tank for pure water supply
1913	Began rubbish removal; built new and repaired old curbs and sidewalks
1914	Operated first public movies in Old Town Hall
1923	Fought infestation of Japanese beetles with a program of spraying
1932	Generated action on acquiring new post office building
1933–1937	Planned/negotiated dams on Hooten Creek, creating Strawbridge Lake; work done by WPA
1948	Financed and conducted research for first zoning laws
1950	Sponsored the establishment of the township planning board
1954	Helped to divert Route 295, originally planned to bisect Moorestown
1965	Resisted removal of the post office from its present location
1969	Petitions circulated for fluoridation of water
1970	Supported purchased of Smith-Cadbury Mansion by historical society Renewed successful campaign against high-rise apartments
1974–1976	Initiated and produced bicentennial presentation, "Moorestown—1976 Past, Present & Future"
1984–1989	Research and preparation for application of Moorestown Historic District to be placed in National Register of Historic Places
1990	Moorestown Historic District placed in National Register of Historic Places
1991–1992	Provided major support to the Save Stokes Hill project
1992	Published guidebook *A Walking Tour in the Moorestown Historic District*
1993–2000	Provided major support to the restoration of Strawbridge Lake project
2000	Provided funds for refurbishing of the banks and floodplain of Strawbridge Lake
2002	Dedication of Then & Now photographic project for town hall
2004	100th-anniversary event: "An Evening at Moore's Tavern"
2005	Designed, procured, and installed 15 Welcome to Moorestown signs on town entry roads
2009	Established semiannual Historic & Architectural Walking Tours of Moorestown
2010	North Church Street water tower gets historic label and tree logos by MIA Windows on Main Street project supporting Moorestown Community House

Visit us at
arcadiapublishing.com

www.ingramcontent.com/pod-product-compliance
Lightning Source LLC
Chambersburg PA
CBHW050702110426
42813CB00007B/2058